I0802044

STUDY GUIDE

Fear & Trembling

The Trauma of God's Holiness

R.C. Sproul

LIGONIER MINISTRIES
Renew your Mind.
LIGONIER.ORG | 800-435-4343

421 Ligonier Court, Sanford, FL 32771
E-mail: info@ligonier.org

Printed in China.

1

Encountering God

INTRODUCTION

There are few people more zealous—and, often, more obnoxious—than a new convert. Whether it is someone who has kicked a bad habit, found a new computer program, or fallen for a new boyfriend or girlfriend, a convert seems to have a one-track mind. His or her new love is *the* topic of constant conversation. If we are patient, however, we usually can count on our zealous friend to come back down to earth, to temper that love with a dose of realism or perhaps even cynicism.

That change, however, can be a disappointment to the convert. He may find himself thinking back on those first heady days of that newfound love, longing for that sense of excitement and satisfaction. The joy of having kicked the habit is gone when the habit begins to kick back. That computer program becomes plodding and unreliable. That young man or woman begins to show some annoying tendencies. All of our earthly loves, no matter how strong they start, will fade as the thing loved likewise begins to fade. Emotions are spent over time. In short, all earthly treasures turn to rust.

There is one love, however, that should never grow cold, for the object of love never changes. That love, of course, is our love for God. When we embrace Jesus Christ and His work for us on the cross, we are changed more radically than we have ever been or ever will be changed. By His grace, we move from one whose greatest good is the self to one who is in the service of the only One who truly is good. And because we are now indwelled by His Holy Spirit, we should expect that our ardor will never wane, that our excitement will never diminish.

But it does. We lose sight of where we came from. We lose sight of where we are going. Worse still, we lose sight of Him. We remake our Maker in our own image. We begin to take grace for granted, and we begin to take for granted the One who has showed us His grace. Though He does not change, we see Him differently. We grow comfortable and at ease. But even though we have peace with Him through the merits of His Son, we should maintain a posture of fear and trembling before Him.

If indeed we have been redeemed by the one true God, we have been redeemed by a holy God. If the God we worship does not drive us to fear, we worship an idol of our own making.

Though the heavens declare the glory of God, we still forget it. We become distracted with the here and now. We listen to those ear-tickling prophets who tell us that there is "peace, peace," when there is no peace. We grow at ease in Babylon, accustomed to this world, to His grace, and we avert our eyes from His judgment and dread.

It is not only the heavens that declare the glory of God. All of creation speaks of the same glory, down to the tiniest subatomic particle. His glory is too great to be contained in the most magnificent cathedral. It is too grand even to be contained in the most awe-inspiring galaxy. His glory fills the dance of the stars and the minuet of the minute. Such is true because there is no place where He is not. He is high and transcendent, but in that transcendence He stoops to this world. He is also immanent. While God has from time to time removed a part of the veil and revealed His holiness at holy times and in holy places, He is always holy and is always everywhere. Every time is a holy time and every place a holy place if we will but see it.

Wisdom, the Bible tells us, begins with the fear of God. If we will see the world as He has made it, if we will see ourselves for what we are, if we will see Him as He is, we will have both wisdom and fear. And having wisdom, we will seek fear. For the wise know that while it is a terrifying thing to fall into the hands of the living God, there is no better place to be. Before His face is both stark terror and a joy that cannot be diminished. It's the only place worth being.

QUOTATIONS

God's holiness and His nature are not two things, they are but one. God's holiness is His nature, and God's nature is His holiness.

—Thomas Brooks

Power is God's hand or arm, omniscience His eye, mercy His bowels, eternity His duration, but holiness is His beauty.

—Stephen Charnock

LECTURE OUTLINE

A. The Bible says that the heavens declare the glory of God.
   1. And yet it seems that we rarely experience that glory.
   2. People have all manner of conversion experiences, but the moment of conversion may be just one of those times when we see His glory.
      a. But even then, we forget.
      b. One year after his conversion, Dr. Sproul had another experience with the holiness of God.

i. It was nearly midnight when he felt a need to get up from his bed and go out.
ii. He entered the empty college chapel, where it was cold and so quiet he could hear the gears moving in the clock tower.
iii. There, in the cold and quiet, Dr. Sproul felt the presence of God the Father.

c. While we affirm that God is three persons in one being, we tend to focus our attention on Jesus.
i. He seems safe.
ii. But He came to reveal the Father, telling the disciples, "If you've seen me, you have seen the Father."

d. After his conversion, Dr. Sproul wasn't interested in theology or philosophy.
i. He secretly read Billy Graham sermons in philosophy class.
ii. Then his professor began to speak about Augustine's understanding of God's power to create.
iii. Dr. Sproul wondered, "What kind of being brings things into existence merely by speaking?"

e. Dr. Sproul read through the whole Bible in the first two weeks after His conversion.
i. He often found himself pacing the dorm hallways, especially as he read through the Old Testament.
ii. Though he had grown up in a church, he kept wondering why he had never heard of this God.
iii. We miss the judgment and the dread of God.

B. Holiness is the reason.

1. Holiness can be described as God's transcendent majesty.
2. When Dr. Sproul was in college a professor asked him, "Young man, is God transcendent or immanent?"
3. Dr. Sproul said, "Both."
4. The story of Jacob's ladder illustrates that truth.
    a. Jacob, sleeping alone in the desert, dreams of a ladder that joins heaven and earth.
    b. God told Jacob, "Behold, I am with you always."
        i. He is always with us as well. But we don't always feel it.
        ii. But that we don't feel Him with us doesn't change the fact that He is.
            1. When Dr. Sproul preached in a time of hardship, he did not feel God was there. But the congregation felt His presence powerfully.
            2. How we feel does not determine whether God is present.
            3. He is with us even in the valley of the shadow of death.
            4. Remember Jacob's conclusion—"Surely God is in this place, and I knew it not."
        iii. Have you ever felt that you have crossed that threshold and entered the presence of God?

1. If you have, you know that His presence provokes terror and dread.
2. In our age, we seem to have lost this fear.
3. But in the Bible, everyone who comes into God's presence trembles.

DISCUSSION QUESTIONS

1. Do the heavens really declare the glory of God? If they do, why do we so often miss it? And if we miss it, why did God make the world in such a way that His glory is declared? Who is the intended audience of the declaration?

2. Can a person really be saved if he or she never has had a conversion experience? Why are testimonies so different? What do they usually have in common?

3. Why do we miss the reality of God's presence? How can we combat this horrible tendency? Is there any difference between the sacred and the secular? If so, how can we tell the difference?

4. Should God's omnipresence be a comfort to us or a cause for fear? Or both? How might we be affected if we always remembered that we do all that we do before the face of God?

5. Why have we lost the capacity to experience the holy? Why do we find God to be more safe than frightening? Is it appropriate for even a Christian to have a dread of God?

2

Holy, Holy, Holy

INTRODUCTION

There was a time when it was considered impolite to discuss politics or religion with guests. The reason was clear: These were two areas about which people felt passionately and disagreed violently. If peace were to prevail at social occasions, it was necessary to stick to safe topics of conversation. One didn't want one's party ruined by a screaming match between Muslim and Jew, Protestant and Catholic, or Presbyterian and Baptist. That rule has essentially gone by the wayside, at least as far as religion is concerned. But have we all reached agreement, or have we merely ceased to believe what we believe with passion?

It seems that it is now safe to discuss God because we have given Him a new name: God-to-me. There are two important reasons why it is always safe to discuss God-to-me, while it is rather unsafe to speak publicly about God. First, because He is only God-to-me, He is no threat to you. In speaking this way, we begin with a declaration of peace. You have nothing to fear, because this is my God, and therefore He has nothing to do with you. If God-to-me offends you, just create God-to-you, and we can have peace with each other.

The second reason we can safely talk of this god has to do with who God-to-me invariably is. God-to-me is safe in Himself because God-to-me is exclusively gracious, kind, loving, and caring. Nobody ever says, "God-to-me is a just judge, full of wrath and jealousy," or "God-to-me is a consuming fire." Why should anyone object to any god who has what we perceive our best interests to be at heart? Why should anyone object when this god just wants us to have what we want, do what we want, and feel what we want?

It is safe, in polite company, to speak of this God-to-me. The trouble is, it is not safe to speak of God-to-me in the presence of the God who is. The Creator does not take it well when we seek to re-create Him. His name is not God-to-me, but Yahweh—*I am that I am*. His being precedes ours, and our being depends upon Him, not the other way around. He is, and He is what He is, not what we'd like Him to be. The Creator is not pleased when those whom He has made seek to make Him.

The prophet Isaiah found himself in the company not of polite lovers of God-to-me, but in the very presence of the one true God. What He found there were angels whose sole job it was to sing of God's glory. They did not proclaim those attributes of God that we find most appealing. The angels did not cry out that God is love. They did not cry out that He is grace. Instead, they spoke of the God who is holy, holy, holy. God is love and abounds in grace. But that love is a holy love and that grace is a holy grace.

In the face of that holiness, the great prophet Isaiah, who lived in a time when everyone knew that it was sheer folly to speak of God-to-me, who perhaps had a greater understanding of the character of God than anyone living in his day, still was unprepared to meet God as He is. He not only could not make God, he himself was unmade by God simply by appearing in His presence. He met the holy God and saw himself as unholy.

If we understood what it means that God is holy, we would shake with fear not only before Him but when we hear anyone speaking of God-to-me. We would know that such language is a sacrilege, unholy. And we would know that because He is holy, He will not abide being spoken of that way. God-to-me is not holy, even if we claim that he is, for God-to-me is a sham god, a make-believe god, a made god.

We need to understand what it means to be created. We need to know our place. We need to know what it means to be me-to-God. We need to know that whenever we speak of God, we speak of Him in His presence. And we cannot keep the peace by doing violence to the character of God, by speaking the blasphemy of God-to-me. We are His creatures. He has made us. And the only option for us is absolute, total surrender.

QUOTATIONS

Let us, therefore . . . tremble whenever He speaks; for if inanimate and dumb creatures are moved, what ought we to do?

—John Calvin

Seraph round about the throne who cry day and night, "Holy, holy, holy is the Lord of Hosts," give expression to the feelings of all unfallen rational creatures in view of the infinite purity of God. They are the representatives of the whole universe, in offering this perpetual homage to the divine holiness.

—Charles Hodge

LECTURE OUTLINE

A. The city of Rome is a study in contrasts.
   1. It represents not only great secular power, but the early power of the church.
   2. It contains the remains of the monuments to both great powers, side by side.
   3. It represents the collision of the sacred and the secular.

B. The prophet Isaiah wrote four years before the founding of Rome.
   1. In chapter 6, we are told of Isaiah's vision, when he was called by God to be His prophet.
      a. That call came in a context of national mourning.
      b. Uzziah, the beloved king for fifty years, had died.
      c. Isaiah saw the Lord "high and lifted up."
         i. Our English Bibles sometimes spell *Lord* with all capital letters, sometimes with only the first letter capitalized.
         ii. This represents the English translations of two different Hebrew words.
         iii. "Lord" translates *Adonai*, which means "the Sovereign One."
         iv. "LORD" translates *Yahweh*, "I AM THAT I AM."
         v. This latter is the sacred name of God, the name He gave to Moses at the burning bush.
         vi. It is this name that the third commandment says we must never take in vain.
         vii. It is this name that Jesus prayed would be considered holy.
   2. Isaiah sees the Lord on His throne, with the train of His robe filling the room.
   3. He sees the six-winged seraphim.
      a. Their task is to minister in God's presence, and they were designed for that task.
         i. With two wings they cover their faces to shield their eyes from the glory of God.
         ii. With two wings they cover their feet, a sign of their creatureliness.
         iii. With two wings they fly.

C. The message of the angels was this: "Holy, holy, holy."
   1. In the Hebrew manner of speaking and writing, repetition is the means of making emphasis.
      a. Jesus often began His teaching with "*Verily, verily,* I say unto you," or "*Truly, truly.*"
      b. In all of Scripture, only one of God's attributes is given in this threefold form.
         a. God is not described as "love, love, love" or "mercy, mercy, mercy."
         b. But He is described here as "holy, holy, holy."
   2. God is so holy that even the posts of the building, inanimate matter, had enough sense to quake in His presence.

D. Isaiah wisely declares, "Woe is me."

1. This is his own prophetic pronouncement of judgment.
2. He declares that he is a man of unclean lips and lives among a people of unclean lips.
3. Isaiah, perhaps the godliest man alive, could not understand himself and his own sinfulness until he found out who God is.
4. We are in the same situation, for He is still holy, and we all have unclean lips.
5. When we see His holiness, only then do we see the depth of our own corruption.

DISCUSSION QUESTIONS

1. Compare the vision of Isaiah 6 with the vision John received in Revelation 4:1–11. How is the holiness of God described in each? Are there any significant differences? What does this say about the importance of holiness?

2. How does your private worship compare to the worship in these two visions? How does your church's worship differ? What is the appropriate function of our worship? Does what we do in worship fit that function?

3. If God's holiness is the only attribute of God expressed in the triple form, why do we hear so little about it in the church? What should we conclude from the fact that holiness alone is expressed this way, and not other attributes that might seem more pleasant to us?

4. How does a clearer understanding of the character of God help us understand the character of man? Does God's holiness have any bearing on our own value and dignity? How then should we treat others?

5. In what ways do we fail to revere God? In what ways does our worship fail to communicate the holiness of God? How can we combat the temptation to treat God casually?

3

Inner Sanctum

INTRODUCTION

We live in a cynical age. Sincerity is seen as a mask for the insincere, and only a fool falls for it. We are jaded, skeptical. Our national leaders maintain their power by manipulating words and images. Bombs are dropped to divert our attention from domestic scandals. Establishment pillars parade as outsiders and reformers. And the media, the supposed guardians of truth, only make things worse. A few decades ago, a newspaper writer was awarded a Pulitzer Prize, the highest honor a journalist can receive, for her moving series of stories on the plight of an 8-year-old child who lived in the inner city and in the hazy world of heroin addiction. The only trouble was that the reporter made the whole thing up. Her moving story was just that—a story.

The church doesn't do much better. Televangelists shed crocodile tears, pulling the heartstrings of their audience, to get them to open up their purse strings. They condemn perversity, only to be caught in the act. Even our Christian pop stars find themselves unable to keep their sacred marriage vows, succumbing to adultery and divorce.

Not only is our culture averse to truth, it's hooked on images. Whether it be on the television, the radio, or the Internet, we are bombarded with information, with sights designed to astound. And all of it is in the service of selling us something. We are overloaded with information and stimulation until all we have left for a response is a yawn. We've been there, we've done that, we've gotten the T-shirt.

It's no wonder we're bored. And it's no wonder that, like real drug addicts, we go out in search of still more stimulation, more excitement, more anything. But we're looking for it in all the wrong places. Politicians lie. Reporters lie. Preachers lie. They have feet of clay, ulterior motives, axes to grind. But even if they were nothing but sincere, what they have to offer is temporal, time-bound. The excitement will fade eventually, so it's probably better not to get all worked up now.

God is infinite. Everything that He is, He is to the fullest. But one thing that He isn't is boring. Preachers can be boring. Church can be boring. But God is not boring. We may think that He is however, because too many preachers are not telling us the truth about Him.

And maybe they do so because we prefer it that way. Preachers can only tickle the ears of those who want their ears tickled. As boring as boredom may be, for too many of us it is better than being terrified. Fear is fine when it is insincere, when we sit in the movie theater and watch what we know are mere actors in a horror movie. But we don't want to be truly afraid.

Fear is the universal reaction of all those who confront, or are confronted by, the holy. Holiness is centered on "other-ness," that which is set apart. God is not a man and is not like a man. He is different, not only in terms of His moral purity but in terms of His status as the uncreated Creator. Man does have things in common with God. We are both personal beings. We both have the capacity to think. We are both conscious beings, moral beings. But what truly sets us apart is that He is an eternal being and we are not. We are dependent upon Him; He is independent of us.

When we come face-to-face with God, we do not come as equals. We appear as the clay before the potter. We come recognizing that He is holy. And this rightly frightens us. As Christians we appear before Him robed in the righteousness of Christ. He sees us as He sees His Son, as altogether good. By virtue of the obedience of Christ and His atoning death on our behalf, God has made peace with us. But we are still to fear, for He is still the Creator.

Boredom should not be our problem. No one has ever been bored in the presence of the holy. And yet, we are always in His presence. We are bored, therefore, because we not only fail to remember who we are but where we are. Let us remember the words of David: "Where shall I go from your Spirit? Or where shall I flee from your presence? If I ascend to heaven, you are there! If I make my bed in Sheol, you are there!" (Ps. 139:7–8).

QUOTATIONS

Fear is stronger than arms.

—Aeschylus

It is less injury to Him to deny His being, than to deny the purity of it; the one makes Him no God, the other a deformed, unlovely, and a detestable God. . . . . He that saith God is not holy speaks much worse than he that saith there is no God at all.

—Stephen Charnock

LECTURE OUTLINE

A. Surveys show that Americans are a very religious people.
   1. However, the majority of Americans do not attend church regularly.
   2. Why do people drop out of church?
      a. One survey of people who once went to church showed that the main reason they stopped going was that the church seemed boring.
      b. The second-most-common answer was that the church seemed irrelevant.
   3. If we were honest with ourselves, many of us who are still in church would express the same opinions.
   4. But none of the people who had encounters with the holiness of God in Scripture found the experience to be boring or irrelevant.

B. Nothing is less boring than God.
   1. Isaiah's response to the holiness of God was not, "So what?"
   2. Nothing could possibly be more relevant to all people, and to all other things, than God Himself.
   3. The only conclusion we can draw is that people who find church boring or irrelevant are not meeting God there.
   4. Some people even complain that their pastor is trying to hide the true character of God from the congregation.
      a. This is our modern form of idolatry.
      b. We strip God of His most frightening attributes and treat Him as if His character is like a buffet, where we pick and choose those things we like.

C. God is holy, whether we recognize it or not.
   1. To understand what holiness is, we should remember that simple table grace: "God is great. God is good. And we thank Him for this food."
   2. Holiness includes goodness, or moral purity.
      a. We tend to think this is the principal meaning. While the Bible does use the word "holy" for goodness, this is its secondary meaning.
      b. The primary meaning is otherness, or set-apartness. God's transcendent majesty is chiefly in view when His holiness is being considered.
   3. Sometimes we call God the "Supreme Being" and ourselves "human beings."
      a. God's being makes Him different, or supreme.
         i. All things that change might be called "becomings" instead of "beings."
         ii. But God never changes; He is pure being.
      b. Creatures cannot live of themselves.
         i. We are dependent.
         ii. But God has the power of being in Himself.
         iii. And He holds the power of everybody's existence in His hand.

c. Some say the universe "exploded into being."
 i. But this is nonsense. *Something* must have eternal being.
 ii. If there ever was nothing, there would be nothing now.
d. Only God has the greatness of being and the power of being in Himself.

D. All creatures respond with fear to what they consider holy.
1. Rudolph Otto calls this the *mysterium tremendum*.
2. Dr. Sproul's favorite radio program began with the scary sound of a vault creeping open.
 a. The program was called "Inner Sanctum."
 b. "Inner Sanctum" literally means "within the holy."
3. Within the temple, the most holy place was called "the Holy of Holies."
 a. Only the high priest could enter, and then only once a year after ceremonial cleansing.
 b. In Christ, the veil is torn; we can come into His presence, but we still must come in fear.

DISCUSSION QUESTIONS

1. If church is boring to people, should we labor to make it more entertaining? Will that attract more of the unchurched? How can church be boring if God is not boring? What habits in our lives make it easier for us to be bored when we should be excited?

2. Do unbelievers really fear God? How is that fear shown? Should Christians fear God or merely hold Him in awe? Is there a difference? Is there anything else that we should fear?

3. If everyone experiences fear in the presence of what they deem to be holy, does that mean that false gods are holy? Are they to be feared?

4. Should we seek to shield the lost from the fearfulness of God when we witness to them? Do we do this? What differences are there between the way we tend to witness to the lost and how Peter preached to the lost in Acts 3?

5. Does believing in evolution have an impact on how we understand the holiness of God? Which is more astounding: for God to speak the world into existence or to adapt it into existence through natural selection? How does evolution influence our view of the significance of man?

4

What Manner of Man is This?

INTRODUCTION

In calling ourselves Christians, we are acting dangerously on the one hand and shrewdly on the other. The danger is vertical. That is, we take a grave risk of taking the name of the Lord in vain. We are identifying ourselves with Christ, despite the fact that even as believers we are very often not like Christ at all. The shrewdness is in the advertising. There is a reason commercials are populated with television stars and athletes. When a famous athlete graces the front of a cereal box, we tend to think more highly of it.

The church never has been the most warmly received group. We have a terrible reputation. The church has caused the majority of the wars in this world, we are told. The church gathers together those eager to judge and condemn others, they say. It is a haven for hypocrites, at least in the eyes of those outside the church. But for all the hatred directed at the church through the ages, for all the anger and vitriol aimed at believers and their institutions, Jesus Himself seems to have received nothing but praise. "Christ we love," the world says, "it's Christians that we hate."

This disparity is all the more odd when we consider what happened when Jesus walked the earth. To be sure, there were large crowds who loved Him, at least for a while. But despite the popularity that came with His astounding miracles, Jesus was a deeply hated man. The scribes and Pharisees hated Him with a passion, spending their time plotting and conniving against Him. The Romans responded to this Jesus with contempt or a damning indifference. The people whom He fed, healed, and taught also turned on Him at the last. Even the disciples were afraid of Him.

Perhaps the difference in the world's feelings for Jesus today can be accounted for by the fact that He no longer is walking the earth. We are not confronted with His holiness as they were in Palestine in the first century. Perhaps the difference is not in us but in Jesus. That is, perhaps the Jesus this world loves is not the same Jesus that that world hated. Just as we strip away from the Father's character all that we cannot stomach, so we have done with Jesus. We remake Him also into our own image. Jesus, though He drove the money-changers out of the temple with a whip He made Himself, would never judge anyone. Jesus, though He called the scribes and Pharisees a brood of vipers and whitewashed tombs, would never show anything but love. Jesus, though He told His disciples to buy a sword before going out to preach in the world, would never hurt anyone. When we ask that ubiquitous question, "What would Jesus do?" we too often fail to ask this question: "Which Jesus?"

Those who walked with Jesus knew Jesus as He is. Though His glory was veiled, He did in fact reveal the Father, and in revealing the Father He revealed His own holiness. As with the Father, when a person came face-to-face with Jesus, he never found the experience boring. As with the Father, when a person was confronted with the holiness of Jesus, the only appropriate response was fear.

If we do not fear Jesus, we should fear. We should fear that we are guilty of worshiping an idol. And we should know that no idol can save us. If the Jesus we are witnesses to in this world does not cause the world to fear, then we are presenting an idol, bidding others to bow down to a creature of our own making. If the Jesus we proclaim before men is not altogether holy, the Jesus who *is* will not proclaim us before the Father. Jesus was not, is not, and never will be safe. Like His Father, He is a consuming fire. As with His Father, we should tremble and quake before Him.

QUOTATIONS

So in love is Christ with holiness that He will buy it with His blood for us.

—John Flavel

I went on with my eager pursuit after more holiness and conformity to Christ. The heaven I desired was the heaven of holiness.

—Jonathan Edwards

LECTURE OUTLINE

A. While the world tends to hate Christians and the church, they rarely speak ill of Jesus.
   1. Yet Jesus had plenty of enemies when He walked the earth. Why?
   2. Mark 4:35–41 gives us a good picture of the reason.
   3. Many well-known opponents of religion have posited theories to explain why so many people are religious.
      a. Sigmund Freud argued that men created gods because of their fear of nature.
      b. He believed that primitive people, faced with the terror of storms and calamities, personalized these forces in hopes of appeasing them.

4. In the story of Jesus calming the sea, the disciples do indeed have a fear of nature.
    a. The storm threatened to overwhelm their boat while Jesus was sleeping.
        i. These men were professional fishermen. They were not panicking over a tiny little storm.
        ii. They were terribly frightened.
    b. Jesus, once awakened, showed Himself to be master over the storm by calming it with the sheer power of His voice.
        i. The cause of the disciples' fear was gone. Their master had mastered the sea.
        ii. It seems that they would react with joy. But the text says they became exceedingly afraid.
        iii. The presence of God is far more terrifying than any mere storm.
    c. We know that there are dangerous strangers in the world, but we rarely know who they are.
        i. And so we make judgments, assessing those in our surroundings and putting them into categories.
        ii. But here the disciples cannot classify Jesus; the process does not compute, and so they respond, "What manner of man is this?"

B. We all have great fears.
1. According to several surveys, the most common fear is the fear of public speaking.
2. But high on the list is xenophobia, the fear of strangers.
3. No one was stranger than Jesus, for He alone is holy.
    a. The Pharisees were considered holy until the real thing came.
    b. They hated Jesus because He exposed their sin.
    c. Their holiness was shown to be counterfeit compared to His.

C. Even Peter reacted to the holiness of Christ with fear.
1. Luke 5:1–8 describes the call of Peter to be an Apostle.
    a. After a long night of fruitless fishing, Peter was told by Jesus where to put down his nets.
    b. When the nets filled to overflowing, threatening to sink the boat, Peter did not respond with joy and gratitude.
    c. Instead he cried out, "Depart from me, for I am a sinful man, O Lord."
        i. He responded with a lament of his own sinfulness and his need to escape the presence of Jesus.
        ii. Peter became aware for the first time of the depth of his sin because of the power and presence of Christ.
        iii. Like Isaiah before him, he was undone.
2. Jesus was killed because of human hostility to that which is not just different from us but better than we are. He was killed because He was holy.

DISCUSSION QUESTIONS

1. Why do people think Jesus is safe? How can we be sure that we are worshiping the true Jesus and not the safe one? How can we be sure that others are worshiping the true Jesus?

2. Do you think you would have reacted differently to Jesus had you lived when He walked the earth? Why should that make a difference in how we respond to Him? If He was feared then, should He be feared now?

3. Could we be guilty of constructing gods to deal with our fears? Could Freud have been right? Are we guilty of believing things to be true simply because we want them to be true? How can we combat this tendency in ourselves?

4. What kind of response do you think Jesus would get if He were to come here now as He did in Palestine two thousand years ago? Would He do anything differently? Who would be His most vehement enemies? Who would be His closest friends?

5

Cosmic Treason

INTRODUCTION

Outside many of the courthouses in our land there stands a statue. The statue is the representation of Lady Justice. In one hand she holds a set of scales, representing the careful weighing of justice. Beneath her feet is the Bible, symbolizing the ideal of law being grounded in the Word of God. While the ACLU likes to take down manger scenes at government buildings, it's not apt to rip the Bible from under the lady's feet. In her other hand she holds a sword, with which her justice is executed. But what is perhaps most interesting about these statues is the face of Justice. She wears a blindfold.

The idea behind the blindfold is that justice is supposed to be blind. Of course there is no justice if the facts are not known. So she is blind not to evidence but to the status of those who seek her favor. Justice is not to favor the rich for their wealth or the poor for their poverty. She is to give her power neither to the powerful nor to the weak. She is Justice, and so she must seek justice with the utmost impartiality. As Aristotle said, "The law is reason unaffected by desire."

We all make judgments. But few of us are blindfolded when we do so. We fail to judge impartially. Whether we are tuned into Court TV or merely dealing with a petty dispute among friends, we tend to judge according to what we like, what we want. And when we find ourselves involved in the proceedings, the whole world must adjust to our distorted view of things. We insist that those who have wronged us receive nothing but the maximum sentence. Our dignity must never be attacked by another. Our rights must never be transgressed. We affirm with our Founding Fathers, "Don't Tread On Me."

When we are the accused, we take a more gracious view. First, we don the blindfold to our own faults. We refuse to see when we have done wrong. If we are forced to concede that we have done wrong, we bring forth all the mitigating circumstances. We cop a plea, arguing that what we have done wasn't that bad, that the victim deserved it, or that it wasn't our fault. We blame our parents, our environment, our victim—anyone but ourselves. We commit the sin of denying our sin.

Our sin, however, is not done before blind justice but before the face of the all-seeing God. Worse still, it is done against this all-seeing God. When David came face to face with his sin, when the prophet Nathan confronted him for his adultery with Bathsheba and the murder of her husband, David responded with repentance. But we see something odd in his repentance. In this context, he penned Psalm 51, in which he cried to God, "Against you, you only, have I sinned."

All our sins, whether they are directed immediately at a righteous God or at the unrighteous men who bear His image, are sins against God. They are an assault on His dignity. It is bad enough to wrong wrongdoers, but we disobey the One who is altogether holy. And we do so constantly.

Philosophers and theologians long have struggled with the problem of pain. How can God allow so much misery in His world? However, if we understood the holiness of God and our own sinfulness, we would discover a far more difficult problem: the problem of pleasure. How can God allow so much pleasure in this world when we, His creatures, day by day, hour by hour, minute by minute, second by second, are in rebellion against Him? We consider pain a problem only because we take His grace for granted, because we do not know who we are or who He is.

Lady Justice, if she could see the way we distort justice, would laugh or strike us with her sword. We are born rebels, who would kill God if we could. We are the enemies of the King who seek His throne, who want His glory for ourselves. And when trouble comes our way, when reality refuses to correspond to our plans, we respond by complaining and grumbling to the King we seek to overthrow. Justice is not blind, but we the unjust are.

QUOTATIONS

Let justice be done though the world perish.

—Augustine

Justice is always violent to the party offending, for every man is innocent in his own eyes.

—Daniel Defoe

LECTURE OUTLINE

A. We are sometimes puzzled or embarrassed by some of the stories in the Old Testament.
   1. One Sunday school curriculum argued that these stories were not true, but they were the thoughts of a primitive and barbaric people who didn't understand God's love.

2. Some people speak of the God of the Old Testament and the God of the New Testament as if they are different.
3. There are indeed some hard stories in the Old Testament.
    a. Leviticus 10:1–7 tells the story of Aaron's sons Nadab and Abihu.
        i. These two young priests brought a "strange fire" into the tabernacle and were instantly consumed.
        ii. Aaron must have been angry and went to see Moses.
        iii. Moses reminded Aaron that God had said, "Among those who are near me I will be sanctified."
        iv. And Aaron shut his mouth.
    b. Second Samuel 6 has the story of Uzzah the Kohathite.
        i. The ark of the covenant was sacred, the throne of God.
        ii. It was usually kept in the tabernacle, in the Holy of Holies.
        iii. The ark had rings on the sides in which poles were placed so that it could be moved with no one touching it.
        iv. But in this story the ark was being moved on an oxcart.
        v. When the oxen stumbled, Uzzah touched the ark to steady it and was killed instantly.
            1. Critics say he merely had a heart attack.
            2. But Jonathan Edwards reminds us of Uzzah's pride, that he thought it better for the ark to touch a man than to touch dirt.
    c. Hans Küng has argued that God sometimes erupts in a paroxysm of rage, as in the New Testament story of Ananias and Sapphira.
    d. We think the Old Testament is barbaric because it lists 35 capital crimes.
        i. The New Testament seems to have fewer.
        ii. But we forget that every sin is a capital crime, as God said, "The soul who sins shall die" (Ezek. 18:4).

B. The just consequence of sin is death.
1. We don't think we deserve death.
2. But even today, high treason is a capital offense.
    a. Every sin is high treason against the King of the universe.
    b. It is our declaration to God, "You have no right to rule over us."
3. God acts patiently so that we have time to repent.
    a. But His patience only hardens our hearts.
    b. We, like Israel in Jeremiah's day, "have the forehead of a whore." We've lost the ability to blush for our sin.
4. God sometimes sends justice to remind us of what we are due.

C. We need to understand the difference between justice and mercy.
1. When Dr. Sproul showed grace to his students, each time they became more bold.
2. First, they were grateful.
3. Next, they expected it.

4. At the end, they demanded it.
5. We grow accustomed to God's grace.
   a. But God does not owe us grace.
   b. If grace is anything, it is not something that is owed.

DISCUSSION QUESTIONS

1. Can we learn anything about our worship from the experience of Nadab and Abihu? Are we guilty of bringing "strange fire" into His presence? How can we remember the admonition Moses gave to Aaron as we enter His presence in worship?

2. Why do we tend to think of things as impure? Why would we act like Uzzah had we been in his shoes? What can we do to maintain a clearer picture of our own sinfulness?

3. Do we take the grace of God for granted? How can we fight this tendency in ourselves? How do we deal with those outside the church who believe that God owes them eternal life?

4. Does God still do the kinds of things He did in the Bible stories that bother people? Does He ever kill people for their disobedience? Why or why not?

6

Fear and Trembling

INTRODUCTION

You are, in all probability, in the process of acquiring an education. Even if you have completed formal schooling, you continue to seek new skills or new opportunities to use those skills. We are a people not only on the move, but always moving somewhere. We are dissatisfied with the present, so we use it to get where we want to be in the future.

Along the way, of course, we grow weary and discouraged. Our goal often seems to move farther away from us the more we think we progress. We feel as if we are taking one step forward and two steps back. We try to encourage ourselves, remembering the wisdom that a journey of a thousand miles must begin with the first step; inch by inch it's a cinch. And soon those worn clichés show themselves to be just that, worn clichés. They no longer have the power to keep us moving forward. So we make choices. We adjust our sights, or we give up. We teach ourselves to be satisfied with less than what we had first hoped for. We convince ourselves that our new goal is more reasonable, more attainable, more sensible, even more rewarding.

Sometimes, however, we are not given a choice. Sometimes, no matter how long and difficult the journey, we are required to make it. We have been considering the holiness of God. We have forced ourselves to consider the great gap that separates God's holy character and our sinful character. We have learned that we are far less like God than we once thought, that He is entirely holy but we are cosmic traitors. We know that the Judge of all the earth must judge rightly. And so we are undone.

The holiness of God and the sinfulness of man are the poles of the message of Scripture. But in the middle stands the cross of Christ. Because God is holy and just, He cannot simply wink away our sin. He cannot, though we too often think He does, sweep our sins under the rug and let bygones be bygones. In Christ, however, our sins are covered. Just as Isaiah had his unclean lips purged by the hot coal, so our unclean persons can be purged by the blood of Christ. When we trust in the finished work of

Christ, and trust in Him alone, recognizing our sin enough to know that we can bring nothing to the table, we hear what Isaiah heard: "Your guilt is taken away, and your sin atoned for." Our unholiness is replaced with His holiness, and the judge of all the earth declares His peace upon us.

That is the good news of the gospel. The journey has been taken for us. But that is not the end of the story. Having found peace with God, we do not sit and wait. The good news must be told. Having heard this declaration of peace, we hear His question, "Whom shall I send?" And with Isaiah, our duty is to answer, "Send me."

We are sent, however, not just with the message, but with the same command that has always been with us. In Christ we are holy. But God also says, "Be holy, for I am holy." While we are dressed in Christ's righteousness, we are still to seek our own righteousness, not as the grounds of our salvation, but as its fruit. Dependent upon His righteousness to stand, we walk forward in obedience. His holiness has been imputed to us; now we are called to make our own. He chose us before the foundation of the world. We are saved by trusting in the finished work of Christ alone. And we will be saved as we continue to work out our own salvation in fear and trembling, as He works in us both to do and to will for His good pleasure.

The Scriptures describe this process, our sanctification, our holy-fication, not just as a journey but as warfare. It is exhausting, grueling, and dangerous. As we wage the war, we must be encouraged not by clichés but by the sure and certain promises of God. We have been told, "He who began a good work in you will bring it to completion at the day of Jesus Christ" (Phil. 1:6). We will become all the more faithful in believing the gospel, in proclaiming the Gospel, in becoming more like Christ when we remember that He is with us, that we fight this grand war before His face and for His glory.

QUOTATIONS

The strength of a man's virtues must be measured not by his efforts, but by his ordinary life.

—Blaise Pascal

There is no holiness without warfare.

—J.C. Ryle

LECTURE OUTLINE

A. Perhaps the most frequent question Dr. Sproul is asked is, "How can I know the will of God for my life?"
    1. No one can tell you what kind of job God wants you to have, or whom you should marry.

2. But we can know God's will for our lives—our sanctification.
    a. Sanctification is "holy-fication."
    b. The process begins at conversion.
    c. But we still sin.
    d. The Bible calls us "saints," or holy ones.
3. We are saved by the work of Christ, then commanded to work out our salvation.
4. We are to work it out with fear and trembling.
    a. This task is of supreme importance.
    b. But we are cavalier about it today.
    c. We think the pursuit of righteousness is no big deal.
    d. But Jesus said that our righteousness must exceed the righteousness of the scribes and Pharisees.
        i. We think that's easy because they were hypocrites.
        ii. But they were hypocrites who were zealous for the law.
        iii. We're not even zealous enough to be hypocrites.
        iv. But Jesus loved the law and obeyed the law.

B. Isaiah cried out that he was undone.
1. We call this "disintegration."
2. How did God respond?
    a. A seraph purified his lips with a hot coal.
    b. Isaiah repented, and so was cleansed.
    c. The angel said, "Behold, this has touched your lips; your guilt is taken away, and your sin atoned for."
        i. Christ is the one who "expiates" or removes our guilt.
        ii. In the Old Testament system, the scapegoat took away the sins of the people.
3. In our justification, we who are unjust are declared by God to be just, that is, righteous in Christ.
    a. None could stand before His justice.
    b. Our unholiness must be removed, which Christ did. And He granted us His holiness.
4. Now we are called to go to work.
    a. How would you feel if Jesus were to say to you: "I'm making you clean. I forgive you"?
    b. God then asks, "Whom shall I send?"
        i. Isaiah responds to God's question by saying, "Send me."
        ii. All who hear the call of God to "Come to me" likewise hear the command of God to "Go into all the world."
5. God is at work in us, cleansing and purifying us, having already declared us to be just.

DISCUSSION QUESTIONS

1. What is the proper standard for holiness? Can we grow more holy if we do not know, study, and love the law of God? What place does the law of God have in the life of the believer?

2. If the gospel is so glorious, why are we so slow to proclaim it to others? And why are they so slow to accept it? Why do some believe while others do not? Are believers better than unbelievers?

3. What kinds of things distract us from pursuing holiness? Why do we judge other things, whether it is golf, friends, or anything, to be more important than holiness? How can we encourage each other in holiness? What part does family play?

4. Is it just for God to declare us to be just when we are still in ourselves unjust? Is it honest?

5. How can we be sure that we do not confuse the holiness we are called to with the holiness that Christ gave us? How can we combat pride that might creep in as we progress in holiness? How can we combat frustration as we find ourselves so very far from where we ought to be?